Tony Judge served in Blackpool Borough Police from 1953 until 1962, when he became Assistant to the Secretary of the Joint Central Committee of the Police Federation. In 1968 he founded *Police*, the monthly magazine of the Police Federation, of which he is Editor. He has written a number of books on the police service.

Police Magazine regularly features cartoons by Patterson – Inspector Graham Patterson – and Jedd – John Edwards, a former police inspector – who have each drawn 12 black-and-white cartoons for this book.

D0928235

'Anything You Say . . .'

Best Stories from the Police Forces

Compiled by Tony Judge

Foreword by the Rt Hon Viscount Whitelaw, CH, MC

Illustrated by Jedd and Patterson

Futura

A Futura Book

Copyright © Tony Judge 1985

First published in Great Britain in 1985
by Buchan & Enright, Publishers, Limited

This edition published in 1987
by Futura Publications, a Division of
Macdonald & Co (Publishers) Ltd
London & Sydney

ISBN 0 7088 3171 0

Printed and bound in Great Britain by
Collins, Glasgow

Futura Publications
A Division of
Macdonald & Co (Publishers) Ltd
Greater London House
Hampstead Road
London NW1 7QX

A BPCC plc Company

FOREWORD
BY
THE RT HON VISCOUNT WHITELAW, CH, MC

I am sure all who buy this book will derive great satisfaction
as well as pleasure. The pleasure of course comes from the
humour and human interest of the stories. The satisfaction
is from contributing to the very worthwhile causes
benefiting from the proceeds – the convalescent homes, the
Police Dependants' Trust, and the Soldiers', Sailors' and
Airmen's Families Association. They already do immense
good work, and it therefore gives me particular pleasure to
wish this venture every success to help them in the future.

INTRODUCTION

'Don't you know who I am, officer?' demands the pampered 'bright young thing' at the wheel of her Lagonda, in the *Punch* cartoon of the early twenties.

'No, miss,' answers the imperturbable bobby, notebook in hand, 'and I'll need the address as well.'

In South Africa, they say that the police go around in threes. One can read. The other can write. The third keeps an eye on the other two radicals.

Policemen have been the butt of every nation's jokes for many centuries. Shakespeare made fun of Dogberry, the bumbling constable in *Much Ado About Nothing*. Gilbert told us of the unhappiness of the policeman's lot. But policemen themselves see the funny side of a job where the laughter, as well as the tears, are never far away. There is a special and largely indefinable strand of humour called the 'police joke', and the two illustrators of this book, 'Jedd' and Patterson, are masters of the art. Often, it is black comedy with a streak of apparent cruelty, because so much of a policeman's work is tied up with the darker side of life and laughter eases the tension. But it is because the police officer must retain the capacity to laugh at himself that the humanity of the job always shines through.

Britain has always enjoyed a special relationship with its police ever since Robert Peel put the first uniformed officers on the streets of London. They are our friends when we need them, and a nuisance when we are up to no good (even if that means no more than parking on a yellow line). But it is

7

not for nothing that the uniformed bobby, with his unique police helmet, has become synonymous with the very best of British. With this in mind, this book is published in aid of those police officers, and their dependants, who have themselves been victims of the dark side of policing: proceeds from the book's sales are to go to the Police Dependants' Trust, the Convalescent Police Seaside Home and the Northern Police Convalescent Home. In addition, a donation will be made to the Soldiers', Sailors' and Airmen's Families Association, this being a special fund-raising year for them.

This book offers you just a flavour of the funny side of policing. Jedd, Patterson and I hope you enjoy it.

September 1985

EDITOR'S NOTE

A large number of the stories in this volume have not been attributed to anybody in particular. This is either because they were sent in anonymously or by several contributors, or because they have been circulating round Britain's police forces for some time.

A STORY I always remember with affection came from the late Sir Derek Capper, Chief Constable of Birmingham:

When I was an inspector in the West End of London, I was patrolling through Soho one evening when I heard screams coming from the flat of a known prostitute. I rushed up the stairs to find her grappling with a most enormous man. Naturally, I intervened; in the struggle that followed we all fell on the bed, which promptly disintegrated.

About a month later I was duty inspector at West End Central Police Station, where part of my duty was to charge prisoners. A PC came in with a prostitute who, as soon as she saw me, cried out for all to hear: 'I know you – you're the bugger who broke my bed.'

MAURICE BUCK, OBE, QPM,
Chief Constable, Northamptonshire

GILBERT HEMMERDE, KC was one of the most colourful characters who ever graced the criminal bar in the North of England. An advocate of the old histrionic school, his speciality was weaving spells over Liverpool juries. Once, faced with cast-iron prosecution evidence, he was defending a man charged with grievous bodily harm. Working himself up into a passion, he ended his peroration: 'Ladies and gentlemen, you cannot, you dare not – indeed I defy you to – find this man, my client, guilty, solely on the

uncorroborated evidence of these fourteen police officers!'
  And, of course, they didn't.

TONY JUDGE

THE METROPOLITAN Police manpower shortage is graver than we think. A Kilburn PC rang the nearby Harrow nick the other day. It was some time before the phone was answered, and then it began to dawn on the Kilburn caller that the person at the Harrow end did not understand much about the police. 'Are you a policeman?' asked the Kilburn man. 'Oh, no, guv. I've been standing here for ages waiting to produce my driving licence. There is no one here, the phone was ringing, so I just nipped over the counter to answer it.'

Police Magazine

SUSSEX POLICE have a splendid system for getting news across to the rank and file. It is called Update, and consists of a video tape which is sent to all stations. When the boys and girls loaded the video machines and settled back to watch the latest tape, the first item was on how to load tapes and operate the machines.

Police Magazine

ENSHRINED for posterity in the Occurrence Log at a South Devon station is this entry:

> There is a man indecently exposing himself and masturbating at Lower Polsham Road. He's been doing it for ages. I think he needs help.
> Action taken: WPC —— attending.

Police Magazine

Some Promotion Examination answers

On Firearms

'Jackson requires a firearms certificate, available from all good police stations.'

'Pierre, as a tourist to this country, does not need to have a certificate in order to use his weapon in this country during his holiday.'

On Hoax Calls

'It is an offence for any person by means of telephone, letter, telegram, mirror, smoke signal, or other such devious means to transmit to the fire services any such message of a malicious nature, calculated to cause public

disorder, insurrection, civil war or the end of the Salt II Treaty, when they are not on strike, thereby wasting valuable time and money (I am not sure if this is the exact wording).'

ONE OF my pet hates during my service in the City of London Police, was the motorist who, whilst I was directing traffic, would creep under my outstretched arm to make a fast getaway when I directed his lane to move. To counteract this, I was in the habit of banging my fist on the roof of the offending vehicle.

On one occasion, during a particularly busy lunch hour, one of these 'creepers' appeared under my outstretched left arm. I adopted my customary remonstrative action but this time the usually unresisting car roof wasn't there. Seconds after my fist had landed, I heard a painful 'ugh' followed by hoots of laughter.

I turned around to find that the vehicle was an open-topped sports car, carrying three immaculately dressed city gents wearing bowler hats. The driver's hat, however, was now being worn at a particularly jaunty angle, so jaunty, that the driver could no longer see.

Ex-DC K. ROBSON,
City of London Police

A WELL-KNOWN Chief Constable volunteered to give an extra-mural lecture at Bramshill. On the evening he delivered the lecture there were only two audience members. The Chief Constable was furious, and on leaving swung on the staff officer asking, 'Did you tell them I was speaking?'

The staff officer quickly replied, 'No, but I'll find out who did.'

J. REDDINGTON,
Deputy Chief Constable,
Avon & Somerset Police

FRANK RANDLE was a much-loved Lancashire comic who was over fond of his whisky. Late one night in Blackpool he was involved in a road accident and arrested by the police for being drunk in charge.

In those days before the dreaded breathalyser, suspects could demand to be medically examined by their own doctors, as well as a police surgeon. Frank insisted on calling out his doctor, who knew him of old.

To the doctor's surprise Frank was furious at being arrested.

'It's the other idiot they should have locked up, not me,' he insisted.

'Why, Frank?' asked the doctor.

''E were reet in t' middle o' t' road,' said Frank. 'Only one bloody 'eadlamp, and 'e made no effort to move over. Ran right into me.'

'Yes, Frank,' said the police sergeant patiently. 'But you do realise it was a tram, don't you?'

AND, WHILST we're on the subject, one 'private' doctor was notorious for never certifying that one of his patients was unfit to drive through drink. Finally there came a time when one obviously intoxicated motorist was examined by him; the verdict was: 'A borderline case, but fit to drive.'

'That's a relief, doctor,' said the station sergeant.

'How do you mean, sergeant?' asked the doctor.

'Well, doctor, it's two o'clock in the morning and I'm afraid that I can't get a police car to drive you home. You'll have to get a lift with your patient!'

'Are you mad, man? He's as p----d as a newt!'

THERE WASN'T a canteen in my old police station in the early war years, the only cooking facilities being a large gas stove used by everybody and located in the cell block. Rationing was very strict, but occasionally a constable would manage a small rasher of bacon for his breakfast, cooked upon the communal stove.

It so happened that one of the firemen from the attached fire station was a local butcher who managed a fry-up of bacon, sausages and eggs each morning he was on duty. This upset one constable, who was a well-known practical joker, and he decided to put a stop to it. The next time the fireman turned up with his large frying pan, so did the constable with a pan containing a small rasher of bacon. They were both frying away when the door opened and in walked the mortuary attendant, in his apron and red rubber gloves, and

15

carrying two handfuls of liver which he slid into the constable's pan, remarking, 'It's very fresh. It's from that fatal accident last night.' The officer thanked him and continued frying. The fireman went a pale shade of green, picked up his frying pan and never used the gas stove for the rest of the war.

F. DRAYTON PORTER, OBE, QPM,
Ex-Chief Constable, Cambridgeshire Police

THE FOLLOWING entry appeared in the Occurrence Book at a police station in West Belfast:

I have reason to doubt the suitability of Mrs Smith for her role as a School Crossing Patrol lady. Today I found her lying on her back in the centre of the road using her school crossing patrol stick as an imaginary rifle and firing at equally imaginary helicopter gun-ships. When I spoke to her she refused to get up until, as she put it, her ammunition had run out.

KEN MASTERSON,
Commander, Metropolitan Police

LORD TRENCHARD, the great man remembered as the 'Father of the Royal Air Force', was once a controversial Commissioner of the Metropolitan Police. Some police officers hated him.

When the Second World War broke out, Trenchard returned to the RAF. One day in Whitehall he noticed a young senior police officer, a product of his Hendon Police College scheme, standing some distance away talking to an army officer. Trenchard stepped over an outstretched rope, strode past a constable who was standing beside it, and walked up to greet his old acquaintance.

The army officer gaped at him and shouted, 'Get back, there's an unexploded bomb here that could go off at any moment!'

'That's odd,' said Trenchard, 'the constable did not warn me.'

'Perhaps he recognised you, sir,' replied the senior police officer.

A MOTORIST who was ordered to stop by the crew of a following police car late one night thought that they were being officious when they explained that his nearside rear light was out.

He gave the rear bumper a swift kick and the bulb lit up immediately.

'There,' he said to the police driver. 'Satisfied now?'

'Yes, sir,' answered the officer. 'Now would you like to try kicking your windscreen? Your excise licence is a month out of date.'

Male caller: I want the police to come to Moreton Terrace.
Police: How do you spell the name of the Terrace?
Caller: M ... for mother, O ... for ... 'orrible ... (*etc.*)

*

Caller: I've locked myself out of my car.
Police: Are you in the AA or the RAC?
Caller: No. I'm in Tottenham.

*

Male caller: I have been watching two people making love in my garden for an hour, but they've gone now ...

*

Park Keeper: I am the Park Keeper. There is a man with no clothes on running in the park terrorising everyone.
Police: Whereabouts in the park is he?
Park Keeper: He's all over the place, but if you seal off all the gates you will catch him.
Police: What if he puts his clothes on before he leaves?
Park Keeper: Oh, I never thought of that.

*

Elderly female caller: Can you tell me what they call those big concrete balls on a chain?
Police: Well ... I don't know.
Caller: Oh, dear. Well, one has just come through my wall.

WPC DOROTHY RANDS,
Metropolitan Police

AN ENGLISHMAN was posted abroad by his company to Lagos, Nigeria.

On his first day at the new office he was driving the company car down a main road and passed a traffic policeman standing in the centre of a crossroads. The policeman immediately sounded a long blast on his whistle and started running after the car.

The Englishman stopped, wondering what he had done wrong. The constable, a huge awe-inspiring figure, glared down.

'What colour am I?' he demanded.

I'd better be careful here, thought the Englishman. 'Er, um, I, er ... black, officer.'

'No,' growled the policeman impatiently.

He made a beckoning sign with his right arm.

'When I do this,' he said, 'I am green.'

He shot up his arm and pointed to the sky.

'But when I do this, I am red.'

AT 5.30 one morning, towards the end of a constable's night shift, a member of the public came to him at the local Queens Drive Police Station in Nottingham. The man had staring eyes, was very bedraggled and was wearing carpet slippers and a raincoat over his pyjamas. He complained furiously to the policeman that an elephant was pushing his car (a Morris Minor) down the street nearby. He had left it

parked overnight with the handbrake on, and now it was being damaged; certainly the tyres were. The PC was not up to the job of dealing with a crank at this time in the morning, so he took the caller's name and address, and tried to usher him out of the police station. At this, the man became even more irate and would only be pacified if the PC would come and see for himself. The officer went with the man, and found that an elephant was indeed trying to push the man's car down the street. Several futile attempts were made to dissuade the beast. Eventually, it was found that the elephant belonged to a local circus and had been temporarily lodged in a horse stable nearby from where it had escaped. The circus manager was called out and was able to resolve the matter amicably. Unfortunately for the policeman, he was known for several years afterwards as 'Sabu'.

Ex-PC R. NIGHTINGALE,
Nottinghamshire Police

SCENE: Discussion between Police and Clergy on a service in Birmingham Cathedral to commemorate the 150th Anniversary of the Police.

Police officer: 'We must have a collection to defray the expenses.'

Senior member of clergy: 'Quite right, my boy, but don't forget to make it a paper one. Ensure that you glue the first note to the plate, otherwise someone is sure to try and make it a silver one.'

JAMES SMITH,
Assistant Chief Constable,
West Midlands Police

PRINCESS MARGARET travelled north to open a new police headquarters. Her host at lunch was the Chairman of the County Council's Police Committee, one of those self-made men who demonstrate the horrors of unskilled labour. He sat next to HRH, monopolising the conversation, and spending the lunchtime on his own legend.

After coffee had been served it was the Chairman's turn to make a speech of welcome. He leaned across to the Princess and said, 'Er – 'ow shall I introduce you? Is it Your Royal 'Ighness, or what?'

The Princess gave him one of her famous looks.

'Does it really matter?' she asked sweetly, 'you've been calling me "love" for the past two hours.'

TONY JUDGE

THE YOUNG recruit, having received thirteen weeks' police training school tuition, followed by two weeks in the company of an older seasoned policeman, paraded for his first shift on his own. He was a little shaken when told to attend a certain address in a city centre working-class terraced area and deal with his first 'sudden death', the deceased being an 81-year-old man.

In the house he found four red-eyed mourners. He was beckoned upstairs. In the bedroom he saw the corpse lying in a large bed. His first sight of a waxen body. Remembering his first-aid training, he tentatively fingered the carotid artery in the sinewy neck to reveal a feeble pulse, and then jumped back in horror as the eyes opened. Still shaking, he said, 'Here, Grandad, I thought you were dead.' 'Nay, lad, Grandad's in t'other room', came the reply.

ALUN CHALK,
Nottinghamshire Police

A PROBATION officer was in court trying to persuade a judge not to send his client to prison.

'He's a good lad who tries very hard to go straight,' he assured His Lordship.

'But just look at his previous convictions, Mr Smith,' exclaimed the judge in horror.

'Yes, sir,' said the probation officer, 'but that's because the police keep on arresting him.'

A MAN with a gift for oratory was defending himself at West London Magistrates' Court. He made a lengthy speech and his peroration ended, 'As God is my judge, I am innocent.'

To which the magistrate snapped, 'He's not. I am. You're not. Six months.'

TONY JUDGE

ASK A silly question … The nice young lady from BBC TV waited outside the National Theatre to get the reactions of theatre-goers after a performance of the controversial play, *The Romans in Britain*. 'What did you think of the homosexual rape?' she asked one person. 'Well,' he replied, 'you sort of have to take it in your stride, don't you?'

Police Magazine

UNDER THE new command structure in Sussex, the responsibility for public order, demonstrations, etc., will be held by the Assistant Chief Constable, Support Services, or as he will be known in future, ACC 'SS'.

Police Magazine

KOJAK, PRESIDENT Reagan, the Pope and a boy scout were the passengers of a private plane which was hit by lightning. The pilot was killed outright and the plane began to spin towards earth. There were only three parachutes on board.

Kojak said, 'I'm the world's greatest detective. I'm essential in the fight against crime.'

He grabbed one of the 'chutes and jumped.

President Reagan said, 'The American people would be

lost without my wise leadership.'

He took a 'chute and was gone, leaving the Pope, the boy scout, and just one 'chute.

The Holy Father smiled. 'My son,' he said, 'I have lived a full life, and I will go to heaven immediately. You take the parachute and save your own life.'

The boy scout said, 'Don't worry, sir. There's a 'chute for you. The world's greatest detective took my rucksack.'

THE MINISTRY of Defence Police, as its name suggests, looks after the country's military bases. Its officers spend a lot of time supervising the entrance gates of such premises, although they resent suggestions that they do nothing else!

The story is told of an old MOD copper who died and approached the Pearly Gates.

'And what did you do down below?' enquired St Peter.

The MOD man drew himself up to his full height and said, 'Sir, I was a constable in the Ministry of Defence Police.'

'Thank God for that,' said St Peter, 'just watch the gate for a minute, I'm dying for a leak.'

IN 1608 the landlord of the Mitre Hotel at Ramsey, Isle of Man, had a beautiful cat with a long bushy tail. It was his habit to let it out on the promenade every night at 8 p.m.

One particular night he let it out and it ran across the

road. A coach and four came down the hill from Maughold and ran over the cat, killing it and cutting off its tail with its wheels.

The cat went to Heaven and attempted to enter the Gates, but St Peter stopped it and said, 'Where do you think you're going?'

'Into Heaven,' answered the cat.

'You are a deformed cat,' said St Peter, 'and no deformed animal gets into Heaven – you have lost your tail. Where do you come from?'

'The Mitre Hotel at Ramsey in the Isle of Man,' said the cat.

'Well, you will have to go back to earth and get the landlord to fix your tail back on before you can be admitted here.'

The spirit of the cat went back through the shades to earth and at midnight knocked on the door with its head (because it had not got a tail).

The landlord opened the door and said, 'You're my cat, you're dead.'

'Yes,' answered the cat, 'I was killed on the promenade.'

'What are you doing here?'

'They won't let me into Heaven without my tail and you have to stick it back on.'

'It's more than I dare do,' said the landlord.

'Why ever not?' asked the cat. 'I was a good cat to you for ten years.'

'I'm sorry,' said the landlord, 'but we have a new Chief Constable in the Isle of Man, and he won't let me retail spirits after 11 p.m.'

FRANK WEEDON,
Chief Constable, Isle of Man Police

Some Promotion Examination Answers

On Licensing

'Under the Exclusion of Certain Persons Act the court has power to exclude certain persons.'

'The father is guilty of the consumption of his daughter in the bar of licensed premises.'

'Tim commits the offence of being seventeen years of age.'

DURING MY probation I was entrusted by the Chief Inspector with a major crime enquiry: to discover the thief who regularly stole a bottle of milk from the doorstep of the inspector's favourite pub.

I was issued with binoculars and told to keep observation from the signal box of a nearby railway siding. Along I went at four in the morning and joined the signalman on my vigil. I saw the milk float stop outside the pub and deliver two pints of milk to the step. From time to time I trained my binoculars on the spot and all was well. However, after having a cup of tea with the signalman, I had another look and, to my horror, found that the thief had pounced whilst my back was turned. I had blown my first big chance.

'Tell you what,' said the signalman, 'the milkman can only be in the next street. Whip round on your bike and get another pint off him.'

I did just that and, making sure that nobody was watching, restored the bottle of milk to its lonely partner.

The following night the inspector called me into the office.

'Nothing happened on the milk job, I see?'

Avoiding his eye and conscious of the colour rising to my cheeks, I muttered, 'No, sir, no luck.'

'It's funny, though,' he said, 'I was in the pub tonight and the landlord couldn't understand why he had got one bottle of milk from the Co-op and the other from the Express Dairy.'

TONY JUDGE

ON DUTY at Ludgate Circus, I heard the familiar ring of the metal-upon-metal sound of a vehicle collision. Shortly after, an irate taxi driver headed towards me.

'I want to report an accident, officer.'

He took me to the scene, where his taxi was in contact with a parked lorry.

I took a look around and said, 'Can I have the details, sir?'

'Yes,' replied the taxi driver. 'He reversed into me.'

'Oh,' I said, 'would you care to follow me, sir?'

I led him round to the front, to reveal the lorry jacked up, with one wheel removed for a puncture repair. 'Still want to report the accident, sir?' I asked.

'Well, guv,' said the taxi driver, 'you've got to try, haven't you?'

Ex-DC K. ROBSON
City of London Police

IN SHROPSHIRE a young girl, whilst at work at her job in a boutique, was approached by a male customer who quickly exposed himself and went out. A WPC attended, after the offence was reported, and asked the girl for a description of the man.

'I only saw him for a few minutes, and the main thing I saw was what he was exposing,' answered the girl.

'Can you describe that?' asked the WPC.

'Well,' said the young girl, 'you could have hung a dozen coat hangers on it.'

JOHN EDWARDS ('Jedd')

HEARD AT a Chief Constables' Conference: 'Has a lemon got two little legs, because if it hasn't I've just squeezed a canary into my gin and tonic.'

DURING HIS term of office the Chief Constable had done the work of two men – Laurel and Hardy.

A CHIEF superintendent went to see the doctor who told him he was suffering from acute depression and an anxiety neurosis.

'I'll tell you what,' he said. 'I know of the ideal little rest home down in the country run by a friend of mine. You go down there for a few weeks and they will soon have you back to full health.'

The superintendent did as the doctor ordered and spent a week of complete rest at the nursing home, which had a farm attached to it.

During the second week, feeling much better he asked the couple in charge of the home if he could help on the farm. They were only too pleased by his offer, and he spent a happy couple of days helping to get the harvest in. The following day, however, the superintendent's doctor got an urgent telephone call from the nursing home to say that he had had a relapse.

'What happened?' asked the doctor.

'Well,' said the nursing home owner, 'he was doing so well helping with the harvest that when it rained today, he begged us to give him a job. So we asked him to go into the barn and sort out the potatoes, making one pile of the large ones and one of the small.'

'Good God,' said the doctor. 'You don't mean you asked him to make *decisions*?'

A BARRISTER was defending a receiver, and stated in court that his client was unable to attend due to injuries sustained with a motor vehicle. When asked by the judge to be more explicit, he explained that his client had fallen off a lorry.

SEEN IN the DCI's office: 'In God we trust – everyone else must be checked through the criminal record system.'

A MAN wanted to be a spy so he applied to the Security Services. When they found out that he had an intimate knowledge of farming they made him a shepherd's spy!

DURING THE hunt for the Cambridgeshire Rapist a few years ago, a special free telephone was installed in the Incident Room to encourage the public to ring at any time with any information which might lead to the arrest of the rapist.

One morning a call was received from a Cambridge

shopkeeper who said there was a man near his shop who answered the description which the police had circulated.

A detective was sent immediately; after a short time a radio message was received from him giving the result of his enquiry. It read:

> The man in question answers the description of the Rapist in height and build, but he is over fifty years of age. He is also a Bishop visiting his old College.

F. DRAYTON PORTER, OBE, QPM,
Ex-Chief Constable, Cambridgeshire Police

A MAJOR by-pass was being constructed in North Wales. One day an Irishman called at the police station.

'What can I do for you?' asked the sergeant.

'Well, 'tis like this, your honour,' said the Irishman. 'I've lost my shovel.'

'Where did you last see it?' said the sergeant.

'On the site.'

The busy sergeant sighed, thinking of how many shovels would be lying around on a construction site.

'I'll tell you what,' he said. 'I'll make a note of it in the book.'

'Thank you very much,' replied the Irishman.

'Don't forget to let me know if you find it,' said the sergeant, and the Irishman left.

Two days later he was back, somewhat agitated.

'Hallo,' said the sergeant, 'have you found your shovel?'

'No, I haven't, and what's more, I've got the sack for losing it.'

'That seems rather harsh just for losing a shovel,' said the

sergeant. 'How much was it worth?'

The Irishman said, '£35,000.'

Gradually, it dawned on the sergeant that the 'shovel' was a JCB!

IN THE early post-war years, all Civil Defence police forces had to contribute vehicles and men to 'mobile columns' which occasionally moved around the countryside on 'exercise'. After passing through the town, the columns, made up of motor cycles, police cars, vans and trucks, all bearing their POLICE signs, used to halt at the roadside in order to regroup and allow any straggling vehicles to catch up.

One fine morning an old lady opened her cottage door and glanced down the road. As far as her eye could see there were stationary vehicles on the road. She gasped in astonishment at the police motor cyclist at the head of the column who was sitting on his machine outside her garden gate. Without batting an eyelid he said, 'Morning Mrs —— it was you that dialled 999, wasn't it?'

A HOUSEWIFE opened her door in answer to the insistent ringing of the bell. A red-faced and rather angry constable stood there.

'I've come about the dangerous dog you're keeping,' he said.

'Nonsense,' snapped back the lady. 'He wouldn't hurt a fly. Everyone likes him and the vicar says he's got such a taking way with him.'

'I quite agree,' said the PC. 'He's just taken the behind out of my trousers.'

TONY JUDGE

AT ABOUT 11.30 one night, the police were called to the Hyson Green district of Nottingham where a man was found lying on the pavement with a lump on his head and a housebrick beside him. He was unconscious. It transpired that he had thrown the brick at a plate glass window in an attempt to smash and grab – and the brick had bounced back, hit the man on the head and knocked him out.

Ex-PC R. NIGHTINGALE,
Nottinghamshire Police

A SQUAD of police raided a pub where they found a fair crowd of customers drinking after hours. The landlord was told he would be summonsed for the offence, and the officers began to take details of the people present.

After asking one rather elderly lady for her name and address, a constable went on: 'And what are you drinking?'

'That's very nice of you,' she replied, 'but I think I heard your inspector say the bar was now closed.'

Caller: I'm locked out of my car.
Police: Have you got quarter lights?
Caller: No, only fog lights.

*

Male Caller: Good evening. I'm just taking my girl friend home and I have run over a gentleman's leg. He got up and said, 'Thank you for stopping', and walked off. Should I go into the police station?

*

Male caller: I'm calling from a telephone box but I don't know where I am.
Police: On the wall under the mirror is a card which will give you the address of the box.
After a long interval:
Caller, are you still there?
Caller Sorry, guv. I can't get the mirror off the wall.

*

Male Caller: I've had an accident.
Police: Where?
Caller: In the street.
Police: Yes, but where?
Caller: By the yellow lines.

*

Female Caller: 'Ere, there's a man on the roof of our flats and he's trying to jump off.
Police: Where exactly is he?
Caller: He's right on top of our roof. I don't mind that, but he's keeping my kids awake.

WPC DOROTHY RANDS,
Metropolitan Police

THE CHIEF CONSTABLES of two large and adjoining forces were locked in polite but bitter rivalry.

One day they were both attending a police conference in London. When it ended, one Chief discovered that his chauffeur-driven car had broken down.

'That's all right,' said the other. 'I'll give you a lift back in mine.'

Naturally this Chief's car was the very latest limousine, equipped with every conceivable extra including, much to the envy of his colleague, a telephone. Car telephones in those days were a new idea, and on the long journey north the host Chief Constable made a point of making several telephone calls.

The next day, the other Chief sent for his staff officer. 'I want a car telephone installed right away,' he said. 'Never mind the expense, get it done.'

Within a day or two, the phone was installed and ready for use. The Chief could not wait to let his rival know that he was no longer one up on him. Out he went in the car and immediately dialled the other Chief's car phone number.

A voice at the other end said, 'This is the Chief Constable's car phone. Would you mind waiting? He's on the other line.'

WHEN a new police house was built in the village, the old one was sold. On her first night in residence, the new owner answered the telephone.

'Is that the police house?' asked the caller.

'Oh, no, they've moved.'

41

'Do you know their new number?'

'No. I'll look in the book for you.'

There followed a pause.

'Hello, are you still there? I've found it. It's nine, nine, nine.'

IT WAS the young detective's first big case. He had arrested a man for indecent assault, and was due to give evidence in court for the first time. The prisoner was contrite and had made a full and somewhat lurid confession of his sexual behaviour.

Rather than rely on his notebook, the young detective stayed up all night memorising the evidence he would give. When the case was called the next morning, he stepped smartly into the witness box, wearing his best suit and a confident expression. After taking the oath, he gave a word-perfect version of the case.

It was when he was reciting how the prisoner had spoken of his 'uncontrollable urges' that one of the magistrates, a somewhat elderly gentleman, awoke from a doze. He listened to the detective with growing amazement, and then said to him, 'You ought to be jolly well ashamed of yourself!'

A SOLICITOR was urging a magistrate to grant bail to his client, but he was not getting anywhere.

'I want him to be examined by a pyschiatrist,' said the lawyer. 'I think he has a Jekyll-and-Hyde personality.'

'This calls for the Judgement of Solomon,' sighed the magistrate. 'I'm quite prepared to grant bail to Dr Jekyll, but Mr Hyde is remanded is custody for seven days.'

A YOUNG village PC was confronted by a furious farmer.

'Did you tell Jed Watkins that if his dog chased my bull again I would have to shoot it?'

'Yes, I did,' said the PC.

'Well, he's done it again. Now, who pays for the bull?'

SUSPECTING that the local pub was selling drinks after hours, a newly arrived sergeant called there late one night. The pub was in darkness, but he could hear voices inside. He knocked loudly on the locked front door, but there was no reply. It took much loud banging and calls of 'Police, open up,' before the landlord appeared.

The sergeant pushed past him into the bar, but by this time it was empty and there was no sign of illegal drinking.

'You took your time, landlord,' said the sergeant.

The landlord gave him a look of pained dignity.

'Sergeant, if I called at your house, I would knock and wait. I expect you to do the same when you call at mine.'

PADDY O'BOYLE was a PC of some renown in the City of London. One day he arrested a man called Dew, and the case came to court. When Paddy gave evidence, he was cross-examined by defending counsel.

'On the day of the crime, had Dew been drinking?'

'Oh, no, sir, I nivver touched a drop that day.'

Ex-DC K. ROBSON,
City of London Police

THE VETERAN constable was showing the latest recruit round the beat. When they reached the local pub they walked round to the back. There they came across a tramp just finishing off the contents of a pint glass, which he replaced on the window sill.

'That,' said the old PC philosophically, 'is what I call the perfect crime. He's drinking my beer, and I daren't touch him.'

IN THE days when the outlaw Ned Kelly terrorised the Australian outback a police superintendent was out in his pony and trap one Sunday afternoon, accompanied by his wife. Rounding a bend in a country road, they were

45

suddenly surrounded by the Kelly gang, led by Ned himself. Within a few minutes they had been robbed of all their valuables and tied to a tree, the gang riding off with the pony and trap.

The superintendent was humiliated and furious. 'This wouldn't have happened if you hadn't insisted on visiting your mother,' he stormed at his wife.

'Well, at least I saved my diamond ring,' she said.

'How come?' asked her husband. 'I thought they'd taken everything.'

'Oh, no, as soon as I saw them I thought of the ring and I slipped it into my mouth.'

'It's a pity your mother wasn't with us,' retorted the superintendent. 'Then we might have saved the pony and trap.'

IN NEOLITHIC times there was a small community of cave dwellers living near Port St Mary. One morning, the wife of the community policeman woke him and said, 'We have no food, go out and hunt.' Putting on his helmet and armed with his staff, he set out.

From dawn to noon he searched for game without success and then on the outskirts of Castledown he saw a snake slithering over a rock. He rushed forward and killed the snake with one strong blow. He was about to pick it up when a little fairy person from Fairy Bridge appeared and said, 'Leave that snake alone. Morally that is my snake; I've been following it all morning, but just because your legs are longer than mine you reached it first.'

There followed an awful argument which ended when the cave dweller hit the little pygmy with his staff and killed him.

46

He picked the snake up in one hand and the pygmy in the other and trudged back across the Island to his cave.

As he approached, his wife, a big woman, was standing, arms akimbo, at the cave entrance. 'Whatever do you think I am going to make with those?' she demanded.

Her husband replied, 'I thought you would make me a snake and pygmy pie.'

FRANK WEEDON
Chief Constable, Isle of Man Police

A COUNTRY bobby had a great admirer in a local farmer with a reputation for being mean.

'Damn clever copper, 'e be,' the farmer once told a neighbour. 'Found six of my sheep, 'e did.'

'What's so clever about that?' asked the neighbour.

'I only had five.'

TONY JUDGE

AN IRISHMAN, reporting his seventeen-year-old daughter missing from home, had become increasingly impatient and agitated as the constable asked for detail after detail of the girl – physical description, clothing, luggage, relatives, friends, money, and so on and so forth – and logged in every single particular. Eventually the constable was satisfied; but, as the father, anxious to lose no more time, hastened to leave the office to go out in search of his daughter, the officer stopped him to enquire if he had a photograph of the missing girl. The reply came at once: 'What would I be wantin' with a picture – hev'n Ah'd know me own daughter?'

SERGEANT D. McNIVEN,
Strathclyde Police

TWO RECRUITS, just back from their initial training course, were marched in to see the Chief Constable. On his desk were their reports from the training school. After studying them, he looked at the first man and said, 'Not bad. Quite a good average start. If you work hard and keep your nose clean, in a few years' time you might be a detective in the CID, and eventually you could be a sergeant. Who knows?'

Turning to the second recruit, he said, 'Excellent. A very good performance. I am very pleased with you. Go on at this rate and you will be a superintendent in no time.'

Then he said to the sergeant, 'All right, sergeant, march them out.'

At the door, the second recruit turned and said, 'And by the way, Dad, Mum says try and be home early for your tea.'

TONY JUDGE

ONE OF the police officers at the House of Commons displayed a sense of humour the other day. A visitor asked him what the latest mass lobby was all about. 'It's the pig farmers here to complain about prices,' he said. 'I'm sending them all upstairs to the Police Bill Committee.'

Police Magazine

THE TOP sheet of a batch of looseleaf pages of amendments to the *Encyclopaedia of Road Traffic* was a page with just the following legend:

Please destroy this blank page.

Police Magazine

THE BRITISH media had been less than impressed with the efforts of the Irish police to find the missing racehorse, Shergar. TV commentators and reporters delighted in reporting 'Irishisms' dropping from the lips of bumbling Garda men. When ITV screened *Search for a Thoroughbred*, a smart English reporter was fuming at the lack of action. 'There's nothing happening,' he said. 'Why at least don't they do a house-to-house search?'

Police Magazine

THE STATION sergeant was making arrangements for the Christmas party and looking for donors for the tombola stall.

'Do you think the superintendent could run to a bottle of scotch?'

'Run to it?' said the inspector. 'If he had to, he would crawl to it.'

'WELL, there's three of 'em, comin' 'ome in this car that they've found. Bombin' along the street, knocked a bobby off his bike. The bobby shouted after the driver, "Didn't you see me?" He says, "I knocked yer down, didn't I?" '

TOM O'CONNOR

A NEW set of traffic lights had been installed at a hitherto uncontrolled junction in Belfast. The first week of operation brought a spate of accidents as unwary drivers were caught out, and a number of prosecutions for 'careless driving' resulted. Among the defendants were a certain senior magistrate and a relatively junior colleague.

When the matter came to court, the case of the senior Resident Magistrate was called first and his colleague, the other defendant, adjudicated. Following a plea of 'guilty' through his solicitor, the senior Resident Magistrate escaped with an absolute discharge on payment of costs. He then took his seat on the bench while his junior colleague assumed the role of defendant and, in his turn, duly pleaded 'guilty' through his solicitor.

'There will be a fine of £50 in addition to costs,' snapped the senior Resident Magistrate.

When the startled defending solicitor protested the Magistrate went on: 'This is the second case of this nature to come before the Court today, and an example must be made.'

CHIEF SUPERINTENDENT T.G. SINCLAIR,
Royal Ulster Constabulary

IN A recent test paper, the following question was asked:

Name five ranks in the police service starting at the lowest.

The following was one of the answers that emerged:

Constable
Sergeant
Inspector
Intendent
Super Intendent

West Yorkshireman
(Newspaper of the West Yorkshire Police)

ON ONE wet and miserable evening a road check had been set up near Beaconsfield, and the officers involved included a very young and inexperienced probationer, not long out of training school.

From the middle of the road he approached a low-slung two-seater that had entered the 'net'. He found himself looking at a very attractive young lady.

'Good evening, miss, may I see your driver's licence please?'

The young lady smiled at him. 'I'm sorry, you can't – I've never had one.'

It was a frank admission and the constable said, 'All right, miss, perhaps I can see your certificate of insurance. I'm sure you've got that.'

Another winning smile. 'No, I've never had one of those either.'

Now this was a situation that certainly had not been dealt with at the training school and the probationer did the obvious thing. With a 'Please wait there, miss', he went along the line to where a sergeant was checking another car, explained the dilemma and, with the sergeant, returned to the car expecting to learn how to deal with such a problem.

The sergeant leaned down to the young lady. 'Now, miss,' he started but then said no more. Straightening up he turned to the probationer. 'If I were you, lad,' he said, 'I'd go round the other side. This car is a left-hand drive.'

Ex-CHIEF SUPERINTENDENT MALCOLM FEWTRELL
Buckinghamshire Police

SERGEANT Jones was a first-aid fanatic. All his spare time was devoted to practising for the various competitions in which the Force First Aid team was entered. It was his favourite, almost his only, topic of conversation and his colleagues at his seaside station were bored to distraction.

One day, when Jones was on duty on the promenade, he noticed a small crowd gathered by the sea rail. They were watching a large man who was kneeling on an inert form on the ground, slowly pressing his hands downwards, then releasing the pressure, and repeating the pressure. Hurrying towards the scene, the sergeant bellowed, 'What do you think you're doing? That's not the way to apply artificial respiration.'

'Perhaps not,' the large man replied. 'But it's the best way I know of getting all the air out of this air bed, sergeant.'

A WELSH constable, Idwal Jones, was giving evidence in Durham and being cross-examined before the magistrates by an ambitious young English solicitor.

The solicitor to PC Idwal Jones: 'Is it not true that you interviewed my client for forty-five minutes?'

Jones: 'Yes, sir.'

Solicitor: 'Is it not true that during that time you sent your colleague, Constable Morris, to get tea?'

Jones: 'Yes, sir.'

Solicitor: 'Is it not true that you and Constable Morris then drank your cups of tea in the presence of my client without offering him refreshment?'

Jones: 'Yes, sir.'

Magistrate: 'PC Jones, why on earth did you not get the prisoner a cup of tea at the same time?'

Jones: 'Damn! He was not in the kitty, sir.'

DAVID EAST,
Chief Constable, South Wales Police

A WILY old detective, when needing legal advice from the force's prosecuting solicitor's department, always consulted the same lawyer, a man who, as it happened, had only one arm.

When asked why he reposed such trust in this particular lawyer, the detective said, 'He's the only one who never says, "On the other hand …"'

THE RECRUITS were listening to a long and somewhat boring lecture from the class instructor on the subject of offensive weapons. He noticed that the thoughts of one student appeared to be far away. 'Wake up, PC Smith,' he barked. 'Tell me, if you called at a house and the door was answered by a man who was pointing a loaded crossbow at you, what would you do?'

'I'd put an apple on my head and whistle the William Tell Overture,' answered Smith.

One night long ago, in the depths of winter, an elderly tramp was taken in custody overnight for vagrancy. The duty gaoler, engaged in a prolonged and exciting game of poker in the canteen, overlooked the regular hourly checks he should have made to ensure the welfare of the prisoner.

To his and the duty sergeant's horror, the next morning they found that the tramp had expired during the night. The body was cold; the sergeant, realising therefore that the tramp had been dead for some hours, laid the body, as best he could, on a radiator. There he left it for a while before calling the police surgeon and hurriedly returning the body to the cell.

On examining the body, the police surgeon, a stern, businesslike man, reassured the trembling sergeant that the elderly gent had died entirely of natural causes and that there was nothing to worry about.

Much relieved, the sergeant asked, as innocently as he could, when the tramp had died.

The doctor looked him straight in the eye: 'Well sergeant,' he said, snapping his bag shut, 'the top half died an hour ago, and the bottom half eight hours ago.'

PC RICHARD STEWART
Wiltshire Constabulary

SOME PROMOTION EXAMINATION ANSWERS

On Poaching

'The constable may also seize any rabbits hung about the poacher's person (these should be retained as evidence and NOT eaten).'

'The local landowner will almost certainly be a JP and he will no doubt want to transport the offender to Botany Bay and hang the ferrets.'

On the Children and Young Persons Act

'When arrested he should also be given the facility of telephoning someone, i.e. a friend or solicitor. Not someone like the Prime Minister or a film star.'

'The Children and Young Persons Act, is it? I'm stumped – see you next year.'

A DETECTIVE sergeant was giving evidence in court to the obvious disbelief of defending counsel. He recited, word for word, a conversation he had had with the accused man.

'Officer,' said counsel, 'do you realise you have just given a verbatim account of a conversation lasting half an hour that took place more than ten months ago, without once looking at your notebook?'

'Yes, sir.'

Counsel smirked and turned to the jury, 'How many of us, I wonder, are blessed with such total recall?' and then he turned back to the officer.

'You must have a photographic memory.'

'Yes, sir,' said the officer, 'I have. I can remember things that took place years ago.'

'I see,' said counsel, 'perhaps you could give us an example of something you can recall, word for word, from even further back?'

'Yes, sir,' said the sergeant, and began: '*Mary had a little lamb* '

A JURY at Kingston Crown Court, Surrey, listened intently to the judge's summing-up. He told them that, in considering the evidence, they must use their common sense. The jury retired and then came back. The foreman said to the judge, 'We have listened to you and studied the evidence, but can we still use our common sense?'

Police Magazine

MY FATHER was a police sergeant. One day he was investigating the theft of chickens from Lord Raleigh's farm at Terling.

Like all good CID officers, he made his enquiries in the local pub, but without a great deal of success. However, whilst in the pub, he heard an old boy sitting in the corner

remark, 'I know who had Lord Raleigh's chickens.'

My father duly bought him a drink and engaged him in conversation, eventually getting round to the subject of the stolen chickens. The man repeated, 'I know who had them chickens.'

After purchasing him another couple of pints, my father came out with a direct question, 'Who did have those chickens?' – to which the old boy replied: '*Lord Raleigh had 'em … but he ain't got 'em now.*'

PETER D. JOSLIN, QPM, BA, FBIM
Chief Constable, Warwickshire Police

THE LOCAL vicar called on a persistent offender who was in the cells yet again.

'You have let me down. Last time you promised me faithfully you would strive, might and main, to keep out of prison.'

'Well, I did,' said the prisoner. 'It took five coppers to get me in here.'

THE CHIEF Superintendent was a man of little humour whose invariable habit, on entering the station charge office, was to reach for one of the thick books in which were recorded most of the incidents which had occurred. He would study the entries and then shake his head and say things like, 'Only six summons reports last week, what are the beat men doing about it?' or 'No "due care and attention" reports for a month. I don't know what the motor patrols are doing.'

One veteran station sergeant grew tired of the 'Old Man's' constant carping. When next he entered the charge room, it was to find the station sergeant poring over one of the books, shaking his head sadly, and complaining to the constable next to him, 'Only two sudden deaths last month. What are the beat men doing about it?'

A LOCAL newspaper, reporting a wedding, stated:

The bride's father, Mr George Smith, is a defective in the police force.

Following a furious telephone call from the said Mr Smith, the newspaper corrected its mistake in the next week's edition:

Due to a typographical error, we described Mr George Smith as a defective in the police force. This should have read: 'a detective in the police farce'.

TONY JUDGE

HEARD on the BBC Radio 4 programme 'Pick of the Week': 'Apart from training sheepdogs, PC Williams makes Welsh love spoons and shepherd's crooks.'

JOAN ROBSON,
Police Federation

THERE ARE many ways of resigning from the job. PC Andrew Webb of Cumbria did it with charm and panache when he informed his divisional commander by letter:

For some time now (5 years and 9 months to be precise), my police duties have become more inconvenient for me to perform and they now, alas, impose an unacceptable burden on my time. It is with utmost regret, therefore, that I have to report that I shall be resigning from the force with effect from 28th February 1985. I am confident that Cumbria Constabulary, which has risen to many crises in the past, will continue to function in my absence.

Police Magazine

SHE IS a young policewoman who, when driving a police car, has come across the scene of her first fatal traffic accident. She has radioed for assistance and is rather flustered. He is the duty inspector in the Hampshire sub-division. He is calm, a stickler for procedure, and not impressed with what he finds.

'Put your yellow coat on, Miss Jones, as I have done.'
...

'Now lock your car before leaving it, as I have done.'
...

' – Er, Miss Jones. Does your car key happen to fit the lock on mine?'
It didn't.

Police Magazine

EVERYONE was pleased when a young probationer brought a much sought-after prisoner into Manchester's Bromley Road police station. Told to fingerprint his prize, the young PC demurred.

'He's got a bad skin disease, Sarge.'

'Then use rubber gloves, lad,' said the sergeant.

A few minutes later, the sergeant found the PC gingerly 'printing' the prisoner – who was wearing rubber gloves.

Police Magazine

CAPTAIN Athelstan Popkess was Chief Constable of the Nottingham City Police from 1930 to 1960. He came from South Africa and was an author of many books on police work. He also enjoyed writing stories for children about his life as a boy in South Africa. In one of these he told of being on a farm on the Veldt when a posse of men rode in on horseback and demanded water. The leader spoke to him; after they had left he realised he had spoken to the legendary Kruger, the Boer leader.

Having written the story, he thought it would be a good idea to illustrate it with a photograph of the great man. He went to the library, but the only one he could find was a group photograph. He sent for the police photographer, a sergeant, and asked him if it was possible to extract the photo of Kruger from the rest of the group. The sergeant said he could do this. The Captain had second thoughts and asked if it was possible to remove the bush hat Kruger was wearing, to get a better view of his face. The sergeant said this was also possible, and as he was leaving asked what Kruger's hair was like and how it was dressed. The Captain looked at him in amazement and said, 'Don't be a fool, sergeant, you will know that when you take his hat off.'

F. DRAYTON PORTER, OBE, QPM
Ex-Chief Constable, Cambridgeshire Police

A VILLAGE general stores had recently changed ownership, and the new proprietor, aware of the notorious suspicion of 'outsiders' in a close-knit rural community, was anxious to become quickly accepted by the villagers.

He had already called on the local rector and had made a donation to the church restoration fund; he had made his acquaintance with the landlord of the village pub and had stood all the customers a round of drinks; and he had met the village schoolmaster and made a contribution towards the school's annual outing.

Looking up the number of the local police station, he telephoned the village bobby and intimated that he would like to call round and have a chat with him, and perhaps discuss security matters for the shop premises and any helpful suggestions on parking arrangements for trades people. To which the policeman agreed.

The shop proprietor enquired where the police station was situated and the policeman explained that he lived in the police house at the end of the village main street. 'Just walk down the road from your shop,' he said, 'and you'll see a door in the wall on the corner. If its closed give it a nudge with your shoulder. Then you go up the path till you come to a gate on your left. Give it a butt with your stomach and

65

go through, past my fowl pen and up to my front door. Give it a couple of taps with your foot and I'll be listening out for you.'

'Ye-es, I think I've got all that,' said the slightly bewildered shop proprietor, 'but why the nudging with my shoulder, butting with my stomach and tapping with my foot?'

There was a slight pause on the line at the other end. 'Well, sir,' explained the village bobby with a long-suffering sigh. 'You'll not be coming empty 'anded, will you?'

JOHN R. EDWARDS ('Jedd')

'I RANG you at midnight to report my husband missing. He's just staggered in, drunk as a lord. Can you send an ambulance for him in about fifteen minutes?'

A YOUNG lady barrister was making a fervent plea to the judge not to send her client to prison. He (her client) wasn't helping matters by standing in the dock with his hands in his pockets and chewing gum.

The judge interrupted counsel. 'I wonder if you would ask your client to stop masticating.'

The lady counsel turned to the prisoner and whispered, 'For God's sake, take your hands out of your pockets.'

DEFENCE COUNSEL was on the attack.

'I put it to you, officer, that you called my client an idiot?'

'Yes, sir, I did.'

'Was there any need for such abuse?'

'Yes, sir. In my view your client is an idiot.'

'Perhaps you would explain?'

'Well, sir. He broke into a house and stole a unique Purdey shotgun worth £20,000 and used it to hold up an old lady and rob her of two pounds. He's an idiot.'

A POLICE dog handler was giving evidence in a West Midlands court of what happened when he tried to get a drunk to go home quietly.

'He just told me to f--- off, Your Worship.'

'And then what happened?' asked the magistrate.

'He kicked my f-----g dog, sir.'

A PC WAS giving evidence in a case of dangerous driving. He said that he was standing on a street corner and the defendant's car drove past him at 50 miles per hour.

'How could you tell?' asked the defending solicitor.

'Oh, I'm good at judging speeds,' said the PC. 'I drive a motorcycle.'

The solicitor suddenly hurled a pencil across the court.

'And how fast was that pencil going?' he asked the startled PC.

'I don't know,' was the answer. 'I've never ridden a pencil.'

A CALL was received at Divisional Headquarters early one morning from a worried male stating that he had been talking to his girlfriend on the telephone. She was rather distressed and had terminated the call by saying that she was going to finish it all and do away with herself, and had then hung up. The boyfriend had tried again and again to ring her back but could not get a reply, and in desperation telephoned the police six hours later.

A sergeant and constable were despatched to the girl's address. On arrival the officers could get no reply and in true style, the door was broken down. A quick search of the house revealed the girl in bed, unconscious. The sergeant could not rouse her and as her face was warm, he decided to give her a smart slap on the cheeks. This met with some success and she gave out a moan. An ambulance was summoned and the officers continued with basic first aid by trying to keep the girl awake until the ambulance arrived. The constable kept asking the girl what she had taken. A very drowsy reply was 'cancer pills'.

The constable continued to try to get more information which could be useful to the doctor on her arrival at the hospital. 'But what kind of pills?' he asked. Back came the

slurred reply, 'No, cancer pills ... cans o' pills ... *pils lager.*'
SERGEANT ALEXANDER NIMMO,
Strathclyde Police

IT WAS a bitterly cold day in what passes for spring in the
Eastern Counties. The Regional Police Dog Trials were on
their second freezing day, with the individual tests following
the first day's tracking exercise. I sought shelter from the
wind at the side of the only building on the large playing
field which doubled as a trials ground.

As I hurried into the lee of the building I saw him, the
archetypal police dog handler. He wore the statutory short,
stained Gannex, rolled-down wellington boots with
off-white sea-boot stockings visible over the top, and no
cap. His hair, which touched his collar, was long enough to
exasperate the sergeant but short enough to escape a
discipline charge. Neither of us spoke as we watched the
next exercise.

It was the 'stand off' test. In this exercise the dog is sent
after a lightly padded escaping suspect. When the suspect
stops, the dog has to circle, threaten and 'stand off' until the
arrival of the handler.

The dog was an ageing long-haired alsatian, about the
size of a shetland pony. When released after the fleeing
suspect, he hardly broke into a trot. He had seen it all before
and knew the suspect would stop. A long 150 yards later the
suspect stopped. The alsatian walked the last 20 yards and
then, standing squarely in front of the suspect, gave a single
menacing bark.

'Stand off,' yelled the handler. Go to hell, thought the old
dog as he contemplated reprisals. He thoughtfully circled

the suspect. The first bite was swift and to the point. It took the suspect on the unpadded right calf, and left him standing on one leg. The second bite was more carefully thought out and was delivered with speed and precision to the back of the left thigh, which was displayed in all its splendour as the dog took half a yard of trouser leg with him. The suspect was still on one leg and bent almost double hoping to save his matrimonials with a double thickness of padding. Would the dog go again? He looked in the direction of fast-approaching retribution in the form of his almost hysterical handler and decided on one last bite. He bit the bending suspect in the only place possible, exposed his nether regions and added the ultimate insult to the existing injury.

I had felt every bite, and looked at the solitary handler standing near me who had not spoken during the attack. He still did not acknowledge my presence, but as he took one last pull of his cigarette, he could not resist a flash of typical police humour – a cross between sarcasm, cynicism and pure wit. 'Barbara Woodhouse says it helps if you blow up their noses.' He walked off shaking his head and smiling quietly to himself.

THE LATE R.A. Butler was a great statesman, but a man of self-effacing modesty. During his time as Home Secretary he was driven to his London home late one night. He said goodnight to the driver of his official car and his personal detective, and only as the car drove off did he realise that he had not got his doorkey with him. Being reluctant to wake up his wife at that hour, 'Rab' went round to the back of the house, where he discovered that the back gate was bolted. In spite of the fact that he was handicapped by a deformed arm, he started to climb over. Just as he was atop the gate, a torch shone in his face. It was a very young and very green constable.

'What do you think you're doing, mate?' asked the constable.

'That's all right, officer,' said Rab. 'I live here.'

'Oh, you do, do you?' said the disbelieving PC. 'And who might you be?'

'Well, as a matter of fact, I'm the Home Secretary.'

'Oh, you are, are you? Listen, mate, if you're the Home Secretary, my name's Napoleon. Come on, you're nicked.'

Rab climbed down and went off with the constable to the local police station. As soon as the pair entered the office, the duty sergeant recognised the distinguished 'prisoner'. Explanations followed, and within a minute or so a police car was outside the door, ready to take the Home Secretary back home.

On his way out, Rab passed his erstwhile captor who was looking distinctly embarrassed. Rab smiled.

'Goodnight, Napoleon,' he said.

ONE DAY at the time of the Moss Side riots, the police station was about to be attacked by a noisy crowd of 800 to 1,000 young people. At the very moment that they were running towards the station, a man, insensibly drunk, was being searched at the charge office counter; as the first brick came through the front window, he was being placed in a cell to sleep it off.

Some hours later – at five o'clock the next morning – the charge office sergeant, seeing that the prisoner was stirring

73

from his stupor, had him woken up, brought to the counter and charged. The drunk was then bailed, and the sergeant took him out into the station yard (where twelve police vehicles had been turned over and smashed, where 76 out of 78 station windows lay in shattered heaps, where debris littered every inch of space).

The drunk's eyes came out like organ stops. 'Did *I* do all that?' he asked.

ROBIN OAKE
Assistant Chief Constable,
Greater Manchester Police

A COUNTRY policeman became a born-again Christian, and from then on never missed an opportunity of spreading the Good News. Calling at a remote farm one day, he encountered the young son of the farmer.

'I want to see your daddy,' he said.

''E's gone to market,' said the child.

'I'll wait,' said the policeman.

He began to talk to the boy about God.

'Do you go to Sunday school, son?' he asked.

The boy nodded.

'Then tell me, who made the sun and the earth?'

'God did.'

'Very good. And who made those sheep in the meadow over there.'

'God did.'

'And who made those bullocks in that field?'

'Dad did,' said the boy.

'Don't be silly, son. God made them.'

74

'No 'e didn't, mister. 'E made 'em bulls. Dad made 'em bullocks.'

TONY JUDGE

IT WAS Christmas Eve and I was late turn. By 3.00 p.m. Hammersmith Broadway was streaming with people hurrying to get home with their turkeys. As I drove through the traffic I saw the body of a man huddled on the pavement outside The George public house. The doors were closed. I parked the car, walked across to him and saw he was very drunk. He was about fifty years of age, wearing a brown suit and black shoes, and Irish. I tried to make him stand by lifting him but he collapsed in a heap again, mumbling something in a deep Irish accent.

I can't leave him here and I'm not keen to nick him on a Christmas Eve, I thought. 'Where do you live, Paddy?'

He mumbled again incoherently. Looking through his pockets, I found his address; it wasn't very far.

I hauled him to his feet and dragged him across the pavement. He was heavy.

I bounced off the railings on the Broadway, then managed to lay him on the bonnet of my police car till I regained my breath.

One last final heave and he was spreadeagled across the back seat, and we were off.

I drove to his address, took a deep breath and then hauled him out of the car. He bumped his head on the door, groaned again, but I managed to get him onto the pavement, and dragged him around a lamp-post, through a garden gate, up some steps where I collapsed with him outside the front door. I rang the door bell and a little Irish lady with an anxious look answered.

'Is this your husband, dear?' I asked, gasping for breath.

'Oh, yes, officer,' she said, putting her hands to her face.

'He's had a lot to drink,' I said, wiping my brow.

'I can see that, officer. He's a terrible man … but what did you do with his wheelchair?'

INSPECTOR PETER FORSTER
Metropolitan Police

UNTIL A few years ago, police houses for the country bobby were often remote, frequently lacking modern facilities and indeed in some cases very basic. One such house had long been occupied in a rural part of Lincolnshire by a bobby of the old school, who neither sought nor wanted modernisation of his police house.

Eventually the time came for his retirement, and a younger man was posted to the area to take over from him. The young man and his wife arrived to view the house which went with their new 'patch', and were somewhat taken aback with what they found. On finding no hot-water supply or full plumbing system, they asked the old policeman how he coped. 'Cold tap in the kitchen gives us all the water we need, and the boiler in the shed soon gets it hot,' he replied.

On finding no bathroom in the house, their next question brought the reply: 'Tin bath brought in from the shed with plenty of hot water from the boiler does us well – the kitchen's quite private.'

To their further dismay, the young couple then found that there was no inside toilet, the lavatory being housed in the traditional brick shed at the bottom of the garden. On inspecting the shed, the young constable observed that the wooden door had no lock or bolt on it. Remarking upon this to the older man, he drew the pointed and final reply:

IT WAS a typical ceremonial occasion in a large Northern town. Crowds packed the pavements to capacity, straining against the crash barriers to catch an early glimpse of the motorcade which was not due for a further thirty minutes. The inevitable thin blue line, of which I was part, lined the road on the inside of the barriers, each officer responsible for a 20-yard frontage. Whether to exercise their horses or merely distract the crowds, mounted police officers patrolled in pairs up and down the road.

I had just exchanged a greeting with a pair of mounted officers who had drawn level with me, when one of the horses broke wind in a way that only a horse stoked up on a fermentation of crushed oats, linseed oil and chopped carrots and with a 15-stone rider bouncing up and down on his back, can break wind. The noise was long and drawn-out and reverberated above the noise of the crowd. Neither mounted officer turned a hair or acknowledged what they took to be a perfectly natural phenomenon as they continued their patrol.

My attention was distracted by a shuffling of my small section of crowd. I turned to face them only to find that instead of a sea of smiling faces, I now had a very empty half-circle of space behind me and my erstwhile community, still smiling, were all looking directly at me. It was very evident who they thought had made the noise.

I swear that the next time the horse passed me, he winked.

LOOKING for a particular suspect, we were making door-to-door enquiries; at one particular house I showed a photograph to the Pakistani tenant who was trying his best to be helpful. The photograph bore the front and profile views of the suspect. The gentleman said, 'I think I've seen *him* before,' (pointing to the full-face view) 'but I don't know *him*' (pointing to the profile).

Ex PC R. NIGHTINGALE,
Nottinghamshire Police

WHEN I joined the Nottingham City Police in 1933, the first thing handed to me was a police pocket book. It was impressed upon me that it was my Bible. For my own protection I should enter into it all the things that happened during my tour of duty, as soon as possible after they occurred.

This was impressed on all recruits, and it was frequently inspected by supervisory officers when they visited you. We had one constable, whom I shall call PC Uppingham, who kept an immaculate book. He must have used twice as many as anyone else; everything was entered.

In 1933 there was still a large number of horse-drawn vehicles working in the City, and it was the practice of the Watch Committee to award officers who stopped a runaway horse the sum of five shillings.

One such award was made to PC Bunnan who stopped a runaway railway horse which had bolted from St Peter's

Church, and was stopped near the Midland Station. A superintendent, who rejoiced in the nickname of 'The Black Knight' on hearing of this, realised that it must have passed the constable on point duty at the Walton Fountain. Who was it? PC Uppingham. Send for his pocket book. It contained the following entry on the appropriate date:

10.35 a.m. Point duty Walton Fountain. Saw a runaway horse approaching me from the direction of St Peter's Church. Grabbed – missed.

F. DRAYTON PORTER, OBE, QPM,
Ex-Chief Constable, Cambridgeshire Police

CALLER: 'I want to report the boy next door for ruining our Ivy.'

'Well, madam, it's only an offence if your Ivy's under sixteen.'

'Well, we've been in the house twenty years, and it was on the wall then.'

TONY JUDGE

A MAN driving erratically down the M1 was, inevitably, stopped, by a police patrol car. The police officer went to him, smelled his breath and said, 'You're drunk,'

'Thank God,' said the man, 'I thought the steering had gone.'

80

Caller: I wish to report a physical disturbance.
Police: A what disturbance?
Caller: A P-H-Y-S-I-C-A-L disturbance.
Police: Do you mean a fight?
Caller: As you will … yes.

*

Male Caller (Hoorah Henry type):   I want to report my car stolen. I was in the car park of the squash club washing my car, when this man came up and admired my car, a red Triumph Stag. I thought he was the car park attendant. He was so enthusiastic about my car that I let him drive it. Now he has driven off and not come back.

*

Caller: There's a man in here and I think he has been drinking. They keep standing him up and he keeps falling down.

*

Female caller: There's a man here smashing all my front windows with a hammer.
Police: Do you know this man?
Caller: I had five children by him.

*

Caller: I want you to arrest my neighbour's dog.
Police: Why, what has he done?
Caller: He has broken the law all over my lawn.

WPC DOROTHY RANDS,
Metropolitan Police

A NOTORIOUS poacher in Derbyshire was known to be taking deer regularly from the local estate of the nobility, and continued to do so successfully until eventually the police were given reliable information as to the time and date of his next poaching venture.

A sergeant and two constables were dispatched to a wood in the park where they were strategically positioned, the sergeant sitting in a vehicle with its headlights pointing towards a clearing, and the constables hidden behind trees – all waiting for the poacher to emerge from the wood.

In the middle of the night they heard a sound of someone descending from the wood, and as a shadowy figure emerged into the clearing, on a signal from the sergeant, the area was flooded with light and there, in the centre of the clearing, was the notorious poacher. Across his back, with its forelegs down one side of each shoulder and its chin resting on top of his head, lay an enormous deer.

On finding himself confronted by the constabulary, the poacher immediately started to shrug his shoulders violently, desperately trying to shake the carcass off his back, exclaiming, 'Gerroff! Gerroff!'

A.O. SMITH,
Deputy Chief Constable, Derbyshire

HAVING received a genuine complaint of rape upon a nineteen-year-old girl in a small country village, the young detective went to interview the girl in the presence of her wealthy landowning parents. To his astonishment, not only could she give a comprehensive description of her attacker, but she was able to show the officer where he lived and describe the car that he drove.

Later the same evening, the officer visited the cottage in a neighbouring village and there, as described, was the offender's vehicle parked outside.

He knocked at the door and a voice from inside called, 'Come in.'

The man, fitting the given description, was lying in bed. He was thumbing through a copy of *Playboy*. The walls of the room were liberally covered with centrefold pictures of naked women.

The young detective instantly made up his mind. This was a rapist if ever he had seen one.

He cautioned him and began: 'At 6.30 this evening a 19-year-old girl was raped at —— by a man answering your description. I am now arresting you for that offence and you will be taken to —— police station where further enquiries will be made.'

'You must be bloody joking,' the suspect replied. With that he threw off the blanket to reveal both his legs in plaster from ankle to groin.

Staggered, the deflated detective asked, 'Well, is that your car outside?'

'No. It belongs to the bloke next door.'

ALUN CHALK,
Nottinghamshire Police

EARLY TURN constable approached station cook at breakfast time and requested a fried egg, burnt black on one side, with a hard yolk and a sloppy white, served cold and stuck to the plate with grease.

'I can't serve eggs like that,' said the cook.

'Why not?' replied the PC. 'You managed it yesterday morning.'

THE STATION cleaner died and, after her cremation, had her ashes swept under the superintendent's carpet.

THE BEAT was so tough that when they had a Tupperware party, all police leave was cancelled.

IT WAS the Annual Dinner of the Newmarket Division of the Cambridgeshire Special Constabulary. The Chairman of the Specials, a horse breeder, called upon a special constable – a local blacksmith who plated the racehorses and was steeped in the tradition of horse racing – to say Grace. He rose, and in a voice which could be heard the length of the Rowley Mile, proclaimed, 'They're off.'

F. DRAYTON PORTER, OBE, QPM,
Ex-Chief Constable, Cambridgeshire Police

THE NEW Chief Constable was flattered to be asked by the local radio station to participate in a Christmas morning pre-recorded programme entitled 'What I would like for Christmas'. He was even more flattered when he heard the names of the other local dignitaries involved.

On Christmas morning, together with his family, he sat by the radio, excited at the prospect of hearing his own voice on the radio.

The Bishop was the first to speak, and said that what he would like for Christmas was greater understanding amongst the nations of the world and peace on earth.

The Mayor said what he wanted for Christmas was greater prosperity for the city and less unemployment in the major local industries.

The local MP said what he wanted for Christmas was stronger links with our European neighbours and better trading contracts to assist local businessmen.

Finally it was the turn of the new Chief Constable, and the local population heard him, to his lasting shame and embarrassment, say in ringing tones that what he wanted for Christmas was a pair of sheepskin slippers.

A DRUNK staggered into a police station.

'Lock me up, for God'sh shake,' me mumbled. 'I've had a fight with my wife.'

'We can't lock you up for that,' said the station officer.

'But I pushed her out of the window, and we live two floorsh up.'

'You don't mean to say you've killed her?' asked the officer.

'No, thatsh why I want you to lock me up.'

Some Promotion Examination Answers

On Scrap Metal Dealers

'A constable in uniform may enter any scrap metal yard at any sociable time (that is if the dealer is there and awake).'

On Drugs

'A constable in uniform may stop and search any vehicle on land, sea or air ...'

'It is an offence for any person to grow a plant.'

ON A Sunday in 1954, a very young naive constable answered the telephone at the old Paddington Green Station to receive a complaint from a woman that after she had hung her washing out to dry, her next-door neighbour had started a fire, and the smoke was ruining her wash. The PC asked the sergeant for advice, to be told: 'Tell her to put a bucket of water on it.'

He duly gave the advice. In less than a minute the phone rang again. Another irate woman said, 'The woman next door has just put a bucket of water on my fire.'

GEORGE HOWATT,
Metropolitan Police.

IN 1972 a court case was presided over by Lord Edmund Davies, of blessed constabulary fame. It showed that Her Majesty's Judges are not devoid of humour when His Lordship said:

> ... he went on to say that he walked round the house, saw a light in the upstairs windows, and he knew this was the girl's bedroom. He found a ladder, climbed up and looked inside. He saw a girl who was naked and asleep. So he descended the ladder and stripped off his clothes, with the exception of his socks, because apparently he took the view that if the girl's mother entered the bedroom, it would be easier to effect a rapid escape if he had his socks on than if he was in his bare feet.
>
> This is a matter about which we are not called upon to express any view, and would in any event find ourselves unable to express one ...

Police Magazine

DRIVING DOWN a country road in Ireland, a commercial traveller was shocked to see the figure of a tiny little man, no more than a foot high, standing by a gate, thumbing a lift. At first, the traveller did not believe his own eyes, but when he looked in the driving mirror, sure enough, there was the wee little man, gesticulating furiously. The driver reversed, and opened the passenger side door.

'D'you want a lift?' he asked. 'Of course I do,' said the little man crossly, 'did ye think I was waving me hand for the good of me health?'

He clambered in. He was dressed in a green suit and wore a pointed cap.

'Excuse me for asking,' said the driver. 'Are you a leprechaun?'

'What if I am?' asked the wee man. 'What business is that of yours?'

'None at all,' agreed the driver. 'I was just surprised, that's all.'

'I suppose you didn't believe there were such people as leprechauns,' said the other. 'I'm not surprised. Neither did I until I met one myself.'

'I thought you were one yourself,' said the traveller.

'Only since last Friday,' said the leprechaun. 'I used to be a handsome young boy, a human being.'

'What happened?' asked the traveller.

'I met this leprechaun, that's what happened. I laughed at him and said he looked ridiculous. He cursed me and turned me into a leprechaun myself.'

'That's awful,' said the traveller.

They drove on and came to a remote village. 'This is as far as I go,' said the traveller. 'I've booked a room at the inn for the night.'

'That's foine for you,' said the leprechaun. 'Where will I get a bed tonight?'

'You're welcome to share mine,' offered the traveller.

Tears of gratitude welled up in the leprechaun's wrinkled eyes.

'God bless ye, sor,' he said. 'The evil spirit that did this

90

terrible thing to me said it would last until I spent a night close to the warmth of another human being's body.'

The traveller booked in to his hotel, making sure that the leprechaun sneaked in the back way, to avoid creating a sensation in the hotel.

Sure enough, the next morning, the traveller awoke to find himself in bed with an extremely handsome young boy.

'... And that, my Lord, concludes the case for the defence ...'

TONY JUDGE

A ROAD traffic accident involving the death of a cat, occurred outside St Mary's Church. The cat was removed to the police station by the reporting officer. A frail old lady arrived at the police station some hours later, and told the station sergeant that she was unable to trace her cat but understood that one had been involved in an accident outside St Mary's Church which was near her home. The station sergeant explained that this was so, sympathised with her and, on obtaining a description of her cat stated that it was similar to that involved in an accident but which was deceased. The lady asked to view the dead cat and the sergeant explained that he must first prepare the viewing room.

He ordered a cup of tea for the lady, went to the station yard and examined the station bins. In one he found the victim of the accident covered in wet tea-leaves, bacon rind and miscellaneous canteen throw-aways. Taking the cat by the tail, he shook it but was unable to dislodge all the refuse about it. He then placed it under a running tap, shook it, wrapped it in teleprinter roll and removed it to the Parade Room where he placed it on the parading sergeant's lectern.

He then brought the lady to view the deceased cat. She acknowledged that it was her pet, and the sergeant explained that he would arrange a dignified disposal. After thanking him, the lady stopped and asked sharply, 'But why is he so wet?' Quickly the sergeant replied, 'We do wash the body in such cases, madam.'

R. GOODWIN,
Chief Superintendent, Metropolitan Police

PC to street musician: 'I've warned you before. Now you'll have to accompany me.'

'Certainly, officer. What do you want to sing?'

DERBYSHIRE Police Authority might care to probe conditions at Glossop Police Station. Over the Easter weekend, a prominently displayed notice read: 'Empty bucket in upstairs toilet regularly.'

Police Magazine

HUMBERSIDE'S Police Standing Orders insist that 'Headdress will be worn by all uniformed personnel when performing outdoor duties.' The order goes on:

Male constables working foot patrols will wear helmets and not peaked caps. An exception to the wearing of headdress applies to specialist units, e.g. Underwater Search Unit.

Police Magazine

A REPORTER rang a busy police station to ask if the refusal of prison officers to accept new prisoners was causing accommodation problems in the cells. The harassed sergeant misheard the query, and when the reporter followed up by asking, 'How long can you keep them?' he replied, 'For seven days. After that they are painlessly destroyed.'

Police Magazine

IN 870, King Orry, surrounded by his warriors, was leaving Norway. As they launched their longships, King Orry's wife, Gretchen, waded up to her knees in the surf to see him off.

'Where are you going, Orry my liege?'

'It depends on the winds and tides,' he replied. 'I may land in Scotland, Ireland, England or even Man. What would you like me to bring you back?'

'Oh, Orry, bring me back my heart's desire – something I have always wanted, a stainless steel sink unit.'

King Orry sailed, and by the grace of God and the wind, landed at Peel in the Isle of Man. After he had overcome the token resistance, and had attended to the local maidens, he explored the town. Walking up Michael Street, he saw an ironmonger's shop. In the window was a big shiny object and King Orry, thinking it was a stainless steel sink unit, grabbed it and carried it aboard his longship. In fact he had grabbed a builder's hod.

When he returned to Norway, the short-sighted Gretchen was standing on the shore to greet him. As he clambered over the gunwale clutching the big shiny object, she said, 'Orry, King of the Vikings, you have brought me my heart's desire, a stainless steel sink unit.'

The moral of this story is: a hod's as good as a sink to a blind Norse.

FRANK WEEDON,
Chief Constable, Isle of Man Police

SERGEANT JONES was a fanatical supporter of Leeds United in the great days of Don Revie and Billy Bremner. The team was on the brink of clinching the championship when, late in the season, they lost a vital home match through a goal scored by the opposing team.

Every Leeds supporter in the ground, including Sergeant Jones who was there on duty, was convinced that the goal should have been disallowed for 'offside'. The referee needed a police escort from the pitch, and Sergeant Jones and a constable took him in a police car to the railway station.

The somewhat frightened referee gasped out his thanks.

'I shudder to think what that mob would have done if you had not looked after me,' he said.

'That's quite all right, sir,' said Sergeant Jones through clenched teeth, 'we always do what we can for the blind.'

TWO BOBBIES called at a lay-by near Bedford to report gypsies for camping on the highway.

On their return to the police station, one of them prepared a statement saying, 'I approached a white-coloured van bearing the index number ONT OW.'

GEOFF SOUTH,
Public Relations Officer,
Bedfordshire Police

A PC on picket duty at the Port Talbot Steel Works being pushed and shoved, was suddenly emotionally overcome to the extent that he turned and ran and ran and ran. Eventually, exhausted and falling to the ground he saw in front of him a pair of shiny boots and creased trousers, whereupon he said, 'Sergeant, sergeant, forgive me, I could not stand it any more.'

A voice answered, 'I am not the sergeant, I am the Chief

Constable', at which the PC said, 'Good God, have I run that far?'

DAVID EAST
Chief Constable, South Wales Police

A COUNTRY bobby, having spent many years in his village, was about to retire.

One evening in the local pub, the landlord and customers were discussing having a collection to buy a present for the retiring bobby. It was decided that this was what they would do when a note of dissent came from George, the local elderly reprobate.

The landlord asked why he didn't agree with the collection. The reply was: 'I don't disagree with the collection, but not one for the last copper. *Let's have one for the copper that's coming.*'

BRYN REX,
Avon & Somerset Police

SCENE: A Midlands Police Committee meeting during a power failure.

Voice of member for Walsall (white), 'James, I can't see you.'

Voice of member for Handsworth (black), 'You ought to, Harry, I'm smiling at you.'

JAMES SMITH,
Assistant Chief Constable,
West Midlands Police

GRAFFITI on display in Reading marketplace:

Eat less bacon, the police force is getting smaller.

ALL HIS friends told Robinson that he was far too short-sighted to succeed in his ambition to join the police force. But he was nothing if not resourceful. He sent in a written application and got a reply, asking him to report for his medical examination at his local police station in a fortnight's time.

It so happened that this station had an Open Day for members of the public just a weekend before Robinson was due to attend for his medical. Along he went to the Open Day and found himself in the Medical Room. 'This is where the police surgeon examines prisoners,' explained the sergeant who was taking the party around the station.

'And the applicants for the force?' asked Robinson.

'Yes,' said the sergeant. 'This is where we examine them.'

THE LATE and much-loved Bill Palfrey, who ended his police career as Chief Constable of Lancashire, was once a detective superintendent in a north-western town. There had been a spate of major burglaries which baffled the police for months, until a man was brought in on suspicion. The police had enough evidence to charge him but, in the absence of a confession, there was very little chance of a conviction.

Mr Palfrey was summoned, and he confronted the suspect in the interview room where he was being guarded by a young constable straight from the training school. Bill motioned to the young PC to step out with him into the corridor where he said, 'I know chummy in there of old. He's never coughed to a job in his life, but, tonight, young man you are going to see the art of interrogation at its finest.' With that, Bill and the PC returned to the interview room, and he got down to business.

Palfrey was a lay preacher and knew that the suspect's mother had just died. Shamelessly he played on this knowledge, and wound up a long tirade in which he had pleaded with the man to see the error of his ways by saying, 'Now, I'm going out for a while, and I leave you here on your own with just this young officer, PC Jones. When I come back I hope you will have thought of your dear mother and what she would have wanted you to do.'

At this Bill departed to join other senior officers at the nearest pub. An hour later he came back and, glaring at the suspect, said, 'Well, have you decided to confess your sins, my lad?' To his astonishment, the suspect nodded. 'Yes, Mr Palfrey, I've decided to get it all off my chest.' 'But, sir,' interjected PC Jones. Bill rounded on him, 'Quiet, lad,' he said in a hoarse whisper. 'You'll ruin everything. I've got him on the hook. Get your notebook out.' Turning back to the suspect, he said, 'Right, this officer will take your statement down. Start now.' At which point the suspect began, 'I have nothing to add to the full confession I have just made in writing to PC Jones.'

TONY JUDGE

YOUNG constable visiting unpoliced island. Conversation with local crofter:

Constable: You'll have the wireless?
Crofter: 'No.'
Constable: 'You'll have the television?'
Crofter: 'No.'
Constable: 'In winter you're sometimes cut off for six weeks at a time. Something could be happening in London today and you wouldn't know about it for six weeks.'
Crofter: 'Son, things are happening on this island today that you won't hear about in all your life.'

DONALD B. HENDERSON,
Ex-Chief Constable, Northern Constabulary

TRAINING examples sent to Promotion Examination hopefuls in Lothian & Borders Police contained the following tasty conundrum:

Les, a housebreaker, sees an open bedroom window in a bungalow late one night and decides to enter the

bedroom to see what there is to steal. Inside the room, Susan is lying in bed waiting for her boyfriend to arrive. Les has not met Susan and knows nothing of her romantic arrangements. As Les climbs over the sill, Susan sees his outline against the street lamp and mistakes him for her boyfriend. She says, 'Keep quiet and come to bed before my Dad hears you.' Les, rather surprised but never slow to make the most of an opportunity, does as she says and they engaged in sexual intercourse. After a few minutes, Susan realises her mistake and screams for help. Les immediately beats a hasty retreat. Has Les committed the crime of rape in these circumstances? Give reasons for your answers.

Police Magazine

THE INSPECTOR in charge of the police contingent at a colliery being heavily picketed during the miners' strike was shocked at the profane language used by the pickets against the 'scabs' as they went into work.

'I say,' he asked, 'who's in charge of you chaps?'

'I am, love,' said a burly Yorkshireman.

'Well, look here, I'm not having any more swearing. The next man who does it will be arrested for disorderly conduct. Is that clear?'

'Right you are.' The pickets' leader nodded.

When the next bus-load of working miners passed through the picket lines, they were greeted with cries of: 'Bounders!' – 'Rotters!'

TONY JUDGE

A KENT constable appeared before his Chief Constable on a discipline charge the other day. Found guilty of the offence, he was ordered to pay a fine. Wires were crossed in passing on the details to the pay department, with the result that the fine was deducted, not from the pay of the erring constable, but from the superintendent who presented the case against him. Why says there's no justice?

Police Magazine

THE KNOCK-OUT Snooker Tournament, one of the sporting highlights of the most recent Junior Command Course at the Police Staff College, qualified (in more ways than one) for the *Guinness Book of Records* in that not two, but three, finalists emerged. The organiser of this remarkable event hails from the Royal Ulster Constabulary.

Police Magazine

THE LONG draft police order went into great detail for the civic procession in a town not a million miles from Greater Manchester. Last to be mentioned was a contingent from the mounted section who would be bringing up the rear. The inspector who passed on the draft for typing, scribbled

104

sarcastically: 'And I suppose PC So-and-So will follow up with a brush and shovel.'

A typist produced the finished order and, yes, it ended with 'PC So-and-So to follow with brush and shovel.'

Police Magazine

A PC WAS given evidence in a serious motoring case which had gone to Crown Court. He was being closely cross-examined on one explanation of how the accident had occurred and was being somewhat defensive in his answers.

Exasperated, the judge said, 'Surely, constable, you are familiar with the doctrine of *res ipsa loquitur*?'

'Indeed, Your Honour,' was the reply. 'When we are in the canteen, we seldom talk of anything else.'

KEN MASTERSON,
Commander, Metropolitan Police

IN HEAVY traffic, a lady learner driver was wrestling with the rudiments of the art of driving. Unfortunately, she stalled the engine and was taking rather a long time to sort the problem out. Drivers in the growing queue behind her were getting impatient (it doesn't take long with some people). A police car was also waiting and politely asked the irate drivers, through the public address system on the car, to be patient – everyone had to learn and, at that early stage, mistakes were inevitable.

After some moments more elapsed and no progress had been made by the learner driver, another announcement was heard by all – 'Now what's the silly c... doing?' The police had forgotten to turn off the public address system!

Ex-DC K. ROBSON,
City of London Police

PERIOD: 1939-1945 War. Memo from Chief Constable to constable at remote island station. 'Come to my attention that you are keeping a horse in the washhouse. No permission given – remove animal forthwith.'

Report by visit inspector a few weeks later: 'Horse removed from washhouse, but regret that milch goat is still in coalhouse.'

DONALD B. HENDERSON,
Ex-Chief Constable, Northern Constabulary

LATE ONE night the crew of a police motorway patrol car stopped to see what was wrong with a Rolls-Royce parked on the hard shoulder. Sitting behind the wheel was a man who, as it soon became obvious, was as drunk as a lord. He cheerfully obeyed the police officers' instructions to step out of the car, and the breathalyser test left them in no doubt that he was well over the limit. At this point, one of the officers said, 'I am arresting you'; and told him to get into the back of the car. This he did whilst the officer took the wheel. The second officer, in the meantime, drove away in the police car.

Just as the policeman was about to drive the Rolls away, he noticed a man, wearing a chauffeur's cap on his head, hurrying towards them. 'What's the trouble, officer?' he asked. 'I am sorry for stopping on the hard shoulder, but it was a really urgent call of nature and we are miles from the junction, so I had to nip down the bank a bit sharpish.'

At which point, the drunk in the back seat leaned forward, tapped the PC on the shoulder and said, 'Who'sh got a very long walk ahead of him, offisher?'

TONY JUDGE

SOME PROMOTION EXAMINATION ANSWERS

Cruelty to Animals

'PC may arrest anyone suspected of committing this offence. One exception being the Queen beating hell out of one of her corgis with a polo stick.'

On Guard Dogs

'Persons wishing to use guard dogs must advertise the fact on illegible notices.'

'Notices must be promulgated in accessible positions that guard dogs are on the premises – and I disagree with this law anyway because it gives licence to any free roaming villain.'

A READER writes to the *Peterborough Evening Telegraph* on the subject of dogs:

> ... there should be a law to control them ... our police are very lax on these things. They just don't want to bother and there is one in Central Avenue that barks all day and all night.

Bet he's not a constable.

Police Magazine

THE OFFICER was most helpful when a member of the public called at Leighton Buzzard police station in Bedfordshire and asked, 'Can you tell me if I can take a dog abroad on holiday?'

The constable on the enquiry desk explained the law concerning the importation of dogs and the quarantine regulations.

'Oh, dear,' said the man, 'I will have to cancel our holiday, and it's the first one we have booked abroad.'

'That's a shame. Where were you going?' asked the sympathetic constable.

'To the Isle of Wight,' was the reply.

GEOFF SOUTH,
Public Relations Officer,
Bedfordshire Police

A YOUNG police officer had occasion to visit a certain family on a large housing estate as part of his enquiries into a fairly minor matter. As he approached the house he saw a very large alsatian dog lying across the footpath leading to the front door. Along with postmen, paper boys and other tradesmen, he'd had some unpleasant experiences with 'dogs at houses' so his approach to the animal was tentative, and he decided not to have any conversation with it. As he walked quietly and nervously around it, he was pleasantly surprised to find that the dog paid him no attention whatsoever.

He knocked at the door as quietly as he could, and had to repeat this twice more before the door was cautiously opened by a young boy. In the meantime, he noticed that the dog had risen from its position on the path, and was now standing directly alongside him.

He asked whether an adult was at home and, when told that the child's parents were in, asked to see the boy's father. On informing the man of the nature of his enquiry, he was invited in. The householder, his wife, the boy, the officer and the dog all went into the house, and the officer was led into the living room and offered a chair. As he sat down, the dog lay down in the centre of the group in front of the fire.

Whilst the officer was concentrating on asking his questions and obtaining as much information as possible, the dog suddenly rose, half sat and emptied its bowels on the hearth-rug. For a moment there was complete silence, but in an effort to avoid embarrassment for the family, and seeing that they were not showing any signs of being unduly perturbed, he continued the interview as though nothing had happened.

He concluded his enquiry and made for the door as quickly as he could.

All he wanted to do was to reach fresh air. He thought that

110

he had handled the situation very well, but imagine his shock when he was but a few yards down the path and the householder called out, 'Hey, officer, you've forgotten your dog.'

JOE MOUNSEY, BEM, QPM
Assistant Chief Constable, Lancashire Police

Judge: 'You have been properly found guilty of theft, but I accept that your offence was aggravated by the fact that you were drunk. I intend to put you on probation providing you give me an undertaking not to indulge in drink on any future occasion.'

Prisoner: 'I will that, sir. I'll even get a job.'

Judge: 'Very well, my man, but remember, not even a small sherry before dinner.'

JAMES SMITH,
Assistant Chief Constable,
West Midlands Police

THE FOLLOWING letter was sent by a firm of solicitors to the Prosecutions Department of a Midlands force:

Re *Regina* v. —— We write to give you Notice of Alibi in this case. Our client contends that, although he cannot remember where he was on the 20th and 21st October 1980, wherever he was, he was not committing the alleged offences.

Police Magazine

IN THE days before motorways, a village PC in Cumberland lived near the only main road into Scotland. Late one winter's night he was awakened from a deep sleep by the ringing of the telephone downstairs. The caller was a distant neighbour.

'Sorry to bother you, Joe. I thought you should know there's a dead horse lying in the road at the bottom of the hill.'

The constable thanked the caller and said he would attend to it. However, he was tired, and it was a bitterly cold night, and he got back into bed. But his conscience would not let him sleep. He knew that the road at the point mentioned by the caller was a local danger spot, and very badly lit.

What would be the result if an accident occurred because he had neglected to deal with the situation? Cursing, he dressed, got out his bicycle, and pedalled through the wind and rain until he reached the spot. Sure enough, there was a huge cart horse lying across the roadway. Dismounting, the constable stood by the beast, wondering what to do. Obviously, no assistance was at hand. There was nothing for it but to try and drag the carcass into the ditch beside the roadway. He spat on his hands, grabbed the tail and pulled. Whereupon the horse shot upright, let out a whinny of anguish, kicked out with its hind legs, propelled the startled PC into the rain-filled ditch, and galloped off into the darkness.

113

JUDGE BEAUMONT, conducting a lengthy trial, was anxious to make progress, and perhaps concerned about how much the case was costing in legal aid. Trying to fix a date for resuming the hearing, he asked one of the defence counsel, 'How are you fixed for Monday?' The barrister appeared surprised until a colleague hastened to explain, 'He said Monday, not money.'

Police Magazine

DEFENDING counsel at Crosby Court (Merseyside) was examining his client in the witness box:

'Did you attempt to commit suicide on the day you were arrested?'

'Yes, I did.'

'And was this attempt successful?'

'No.'

Police Magazine

A PARTY of Liverpool Football Club supporters were being taken by coach to watch their team play their great rivals Nottingham Forest. The driver was unsure of his way to the ground and slowed down near a busy crossroads manned by a member of the Nottinghamshire Constabulary. A Liverpudlian leaned out of the window and shouted, 'Which way to the ground?'

The officer gave some rather complex and difficult instructions, as a result of which the bus drove round in a slow circle until it came upon the same crossroads and the same officer.

The same Liverpudlian leaned out of the same window and shouted, 'Eh! No wonder your lot couldn't catch Robin Hood.'

J. REDDINGTON,
Deputy Chief Constable,
Avon & Somerset Police

WALLY BENNETT, cleaner at the Police Headquarters of a small and now extinct police force, was as deaf as a post. Each morning he was to be found with a mop and bucket cleaning the passage outside the Chief Constable's office.

Only once a year was the Chief seen in police uniform, the annual inspection by Her Majesty's Inspector of Constabulary. On the morning of such a day, the Chief opened his door. He was wearing full uniform but his shoes were in his hand. Being a man of few words, and even less courtesy, he tossed his shoes down the passage and said, 'Give these a bit of a shine, Bennett.' Wally looked up from his mopping duties, saw the Chief standing in the doorway and the black shoes on the floor beside him. In some surprise he said, 'Thank you very much, sir.'

Some ten minutes later, the Chief, still in his stockinged feet, saw the HMI's car drawing up outside his office. He dashed through the door and bellowed at Wally who, by this time, was at the other end of the passage. 'Bennett, those

shoes!' Wally looked up. 'They are very comfortable,' he said, 'thank you very much.'

TONY JUDGE

A POLICE constable visited an address in West London to obtain a written witness statement from the occupant. During the course of the enquiry, the officer noticed a large and hairy spider cross the carpet in front of them. Without hesitation he rose to his feet, said, 'Don't worry, leave this to me', strode towards the beast and crushed it under his size-ten boots. 'What have you done!' cried the occupant, 'He's my prize pet and cost me £200.' The interview ended at this point.

R. GOODWIN,
Chief Superintendent, Metropolitan Police

SOME PROMOTION EXAMINATION ANSWERS

On Livestock Worrying

'The person in charge of the dog may show that it was under the influence of drugs which made the dog lose control of its good senses.'

'White has a defence where he is able to prove that the

117

dog (which was worrying hens) acted in self-defence.'

On Discipline

'An affair with a businessman's wife is having a business interest without the prior knowledge of the chief constable.'

THE FIRST arrests in connection with the Great Train Robbery in Buckinghamshire, on 8 August 1963, were made six days later when the police at Bournemouth (then in Hampshire) detained two men in possession of a large sum of money.

The two senior detectives leading the hunt were soon in Bournemouth to interview the men; each questioned a suspect separately.

During one of these interviews, the suspect suddenly told his questioner that he was concerned about a key which, on arrest, he had concealed in a somewhat intimate part of his body and which had not re-appeared. Those were not the words he used, but his meaning was quite clear.

In answer to the somewhat sceptical CID man's questions, the suspect explained that the key was that of a Bournemouth flat the two men had rented, that more money was in the flat and he had thought his action in concealing the key might hide any connection between the men and the flat.

There was only one way to test this story, and the detective asked for the attendance of the local police surgeon, who soon appeared. The prisoner was placed on a casualty trolley in what may be termed the foetal position, the doctor donned rubber gloves, and after a very short time, with a 'Here it is', produced a Yale key.

At the subsequent Great Train Robbery trial, the senior prosecuting counsel, a Pickwickian man in appearance and with a marked sense of humour, decided that first-hand evidence of the recovery of the key should be given, and in time he called the Bournemouth doctor.

As the court usher opened the door and called, 'Doctor ——, please', the prosecuting counsel turned to one of the many defending counsel, and in a voice obviously and mischievously pitched so that it could be heard almost all over the court, announced, 'This is the key witness.'

Ex-Chief Superintendent Malcolm Fewtrell
Buckinghamshire Police

Fred was a Yorkshire bobby who displayed all the financial caution of men born in the county of broad acres. After thirty-odd years in the job, he announced that he was retiring. The custom was to have a 'little do' in the police club, where friends and colleagues would say farewell and make presentations bought with the station collection.

Fred went to see the steward of the police club.

'I suppose I'll have to put some food on,' he conceded.

'Well,' said the steward, 'I can do you a buffet. Would you want the one at one-pound-fifty, or the better one at two quid?'

'What do I get for the one-fifty?' asked Fred quickly.

'Oh, a few sandwiches and a sausages roll, and bits and pieces,' said the steward.

'That'll do all right,' said Fred emphatically.

'Right,' said the steward. 'How many will it be for, then?'

Realisation dawned on Fred and he looked dismayed.

'Does that mean it'll be one-pound-fifty *each*?'

A CHIEF CONSTABLE was looking down in the dumps as his deputy came into his office.

'What's the matter, sir?'

'I've just seen the MO. He says I've got to take these tablets, one a day, for the rest of my life.'

'Well, that's not so bad, sir.'

'Not so bad – he's only given me four.'

TONY JUDGE

THE CHESHIRE Police Drug Squad hit on a brilliant idea for keeping observation on suspects. They dressed one of their officers as a policeman in full uniform, and sat him in a traffic car with another officer. It worked. The only snag was that when police colleagues saw the detective in uniform, they asked him if he had been a naughty boy.

Police Magazine

SCENE: Conference to discuss a visit of Her Majesty the Queen to Birmingham Airport.

Question: 'What are the contingency plans if MAGLEF

[Magnetic Elevated Railway] breaks down with Queen on board?'

Response: 'A long ladder and a bloody great blind.'

JAMES SMITH,
Assistant Chief Constable,
West Midlands Police

A DETECTIVE constable had a good friend who had made a personal fortune and lived in sumptuous luxury. One day, the tycoon told his police friend that he was going off for a few weeks in Hawaii. Whilst he was away, would the constable mind keeping an eye on his mansion?

'Make yourself at home,' he said. 'If you fancy taking the Roller out for a spin, feel free.'

The officer took him at his word, and turned up at the police station one morning in the magnificent Silver Cloud.

His first assignment was to visit the scene of a break-in on an industrial estate. The owner of the premises saw the Rolls-Royce park outside his window and the officer alight. A moment later, his secretary announced that 'Constable —— is here to see about the burglary,' and in walked the driver of the Rolls.

The astonished manager could talk of little else besides the fact that he had always dreamed of the day when he would own such a vehicle. For a minute or so, the two exchanged superlatives about the queen of automobiles.

'Well, let's get down to business,' said the constable, eventually. 'What was stolen in the break-in?'

'A word processor, worth about two thousand quid,' said the factory owner.

'Is that all?' asked the constable, making a note in his book.

'All!' exploded the manager, glaring at the policeman and then at the car outside his window. 'It might not be much to someone like you, but two thousand quid is a bloody fortune to me.'

TONY JUDGE

ON THE first Sunday after I had been appointed Chief Constable of Pembrokeshire, I attended the local church for the morning service. I sat in the second row, and there was another man in front of me. To my dismay, when the service began, the whole proceedings were in Welsh and so, to avoid displaying my ignorance, I decided to copy the man in front. Throughout the service, when he stood up, I stood up; all went well.

Then the parson got into the pulpit and said something Welsh. The man in the front row stood up; so I stood up. A subdued titter ran round the church. Looking round I saw we were the only two persons standing up and, in some embarrassment, I sat down.

Later, when introducing myself to the parson, I tactfully enquired what had happened when the two of us had been standing up on our own among the congregation. He said, 'Oh I was announcing that there would be a christening the following Sunday, and I asked the proud father to stand up.'

ALAN GOODSON,
Chief Constable, Leicestershire Police

Caller (A very well spoken lady):   Would you send the police to Pampisford Road?
Police: How do you spell the name of the road?
Caller: Good Heavens, surely you can spell Pampisford?
Police: I'm sorry, but would you spell it please?
Caller: Oh, well. P-A-M as in Pam. P-I-S as ... Oh goodness me, you know how to spell it.

*

Female caller: I want to report me under-age schoolboy missing.
Police: What do you mean, 'under-age'?
Caller: He ain't old enough to go to school yet.

*

Female caller: Get the police down here quick.
Police: What's the trouble?
Caller: Never mind the trouble, me husband's in a fight and he sure ain't winning.

*

Caller: Could you come, please?
Police: Where to?

Caller:	Bastion Road.
Police:	How do you spell it?
Caller:	Well, call it Plumstead Road, then.
Police:	Is that SE2?
Caller:	We call it SE2 but it is Abbey Wood.
Police:	Is it SE2?
Caller:	Well, we call it that.
Police:	What has happened?
Caller:	It's an accident there.
Police:	Is anyone hurt?
Caller (*bright and cheerful*):	Oh, yes.
Police:	Has an ambulance been called?
Caller:	Oh, yes, they are taking him to hospital.
Police:	Do you know which hospital?
Caller:	No, the ambulance hasn't come yet.

*

Caller: I live in the Borough of SE1 which is in London. It is an area of high-density population and offices with deprived ethnic housing mainly, and there has been a burglar alarm ringing all night.

WPC DOROTHY RANDS,
Metropolitan Police

PERHAPS co-operation between the uniform branch and the CID is not always what it should be. In Dorset, for example, a beat constable at Christchurch recently sent this brotherly memo to the CID office:

I was out on mobile patrol last night, and being alert as ever we noticed that the rack of jeans in the shop that was

screwed by the 'Irish postman', was very close to the letter box. In order to see just how close, I reached through the letter box and confirmed that I could reach the jeans.

It wasn't until I scratched my chin with the offending hand that marker dye was discovered. If this is your handiwork, it will need repainting. If not, please liaise with the shop and find out what they are up to.

Police Magazine

A LITTLE bit of pageantry on Merseyside created some embarrassment for PC Luther-Davies. He was acting as motorcycle escort for the High Court judges' limousine. When the judge and the high sheriff emerged in their splendid regalia from the judges' residence, the PC saw, to his horror, that the high sheriff had forgotten to fasten his braces, which were dangling below his tunic. He stepped forward, and out of the corner of his mouth muttered, 'Excuse me, sir, but your braces are undone.' To which the high sheriff replied, 'Thank you, officer, they are not my braces, that's where I hang my sword.'

Police Magazine

THE NATIONAL Westminster Bank provides a special banking service at the Police Federation's Conference. A delegate called at their booth at 10 a.m. Two very nice young ladies were sitting in the dark. 'Sorry,' said one, 'we're not open until half-past ten – we have no money.'

'I don't want to draw money out,' said the delegate, 'I want to pay some in.'

'How much?'

'Three hundred and fifty pounds.'

'Sorry,' said the girl, 'we can't take it. We do not have a security guard.'

Police Magazine

THE MEDICAL superintendent of a North Wales mental institution was anxious to allay public anxieties after a dangerous patient had escaped. He told the Press: 'He's not a menace to the public. He only attacks police officers.'

Police Magazine

Some Promotion Examination Answers

On Mental Health

'... any person who he knows or reasonably suspects to be suffering from any kind of mental illness (i.e. attempting to pass this exam).'

And Finally ...

'I have read the questions carefully from 1 to 7 and I cannot find one that I can even begin to answer, therefore I do not wish to waste your time or mine any further.'